DEAR READER

This Book

Is A

GRAPHIC

STORY BOARD

OF THE

R E C O R D S

Left Behind By

ANCIENT EXPLORERS

This is NOT in an

ACADEMIC or LITERARY

FORMAT

but the pictures

tell the story

Sincerely,

Warren W. Dexter

ETRUSCAN EXPLORERS

By

Warren W. Dexter

Ed. By Robert J. Dexter

ISBN # 0-9769178-0-7

LIBRARY of CONGRESS
Card Catalogue # 2005930917

Contents

INTRODUCTION

TO

ETRUSCAN EXPLORERS

Prior to the Christian era numerous cultures evolved from small groups of humans gathering in enclaves usually on prominent protective areas. This is how the 12 city-states of Etruria in what is now known as central ITALY were located. This evolution began about or prior to the 9th century BC (Before the Christian Era). The general area covered is from the Poe River near Rome in the south to approximately where the Arno River or Pisa in the North is located. This area extending generally East and covered the central part of the Italian Peninsula.

Just where this culture eventually called ETRUSCANS originated from has not been definitely determined, though several historians have strong opinions. Because little of literary value of the Etruscan alphabet and language has survived except on burial monuments no final determination of their original source has been concluded.

The Etruscan culture has largely been evaluated by its TOMBS, GRAVES, memorial goods such as HUT URNS and VASES and other pieces of ART. Another valued asset in COMMUNICATING the story is their SCULPTURES. The Etruscans were noted for their sculptures and the beautiful MARBLE resources they used.

The 12 City States grew stronger with the assets from the land such as the agriculture resources of grapes, olives, wheat, and the mineral resources and also the resources from the Adriatic Sea on the east and the expansive Mediterranean on the South and West. The fish and general trade industries made the Etruscans strong enough to compete with the Phoenicia and Greeks. Gradually the 12 City States consolidated to become a nation, Etruria.

ETRURIA survived through WARS, amongst themselves and against outsider until the more aggressive southern Romans conquered them in the late B.C. era. Though the Romans conquered the land, the first two leaders of the consolidated new Roman area were ETRUSCAN.

24th January 2005

PROBIBILITY

No matter where Christopher Columbus was born, whether as some researchers have claimed, on the islands of *Majorca, or Corsica* or *Sardinia* or Sicily or Catalan or at *Genoa, Italy* as the Italians claim, Columbus was an inquisitive sailor.

Since most historians agree that Columbus sailed North to Ireland to study Saint Brendan's history of sailing West across the Atlantic in the first century A.D. ***what would restrain Columbus's inquisitiveness from searching into*** *ancient* sea legends of the neighboring Etruscan explorers?

Columbus used the Canary Islands as a reprovisioning station before proceeding to explore the West. ***This practice follows the example of many peoples including the Etruscan explorers who proceeded the Mauretanians on their journeys west.***

The author,
Warren W. Dexter

NO MATTER

the changes

of **TIME**

or the loss of

LANGUAGES

The

I M A G E S

of this book

will be readable

BY ALL

future GENERATIONS.

MEMORIAL

On a trip through the Iberian Peninsula (Spain and Portugal) via bus my camera was constantly on the ready. The longer than normal focal length lens was set at infinity. I kept an eye out for anything of ancient cultural remains.

In Portugal, near Giardia, this beautiful Monumental DOLMEN appeared out in the middle of a mature wheat field. It had three upright supporting stones toped with a large flat stone some times called a "Table Stone."

Because of its location, size and construction it could be assumed that this dolmen was originally constructed as a family tomb.

Dolmen in Guiarda, Portugal

MEMORIAL

This outstanding Memorial DOLMEN was photographed by Mrs. Ruth Hamblett of New Hampshire sometime in the recent past. I purchased it with rights to reproduce.

This Dolmen is located in the Republic of South Africa, North of Capetown, in the Kagga Gamma Park. This dolmen was in the plains country or on a high promontory.

The unusual lighting indicates it was either taken early in the morning just after sunrise or late in the day just prior to sunset.

You can observe several support stones and beneath it all is the repository for the remains. The size of the huge top stone indicates a figure of prominence or a large family of distinction.

Dolmen in South Africa photographed by Ruth Hamblett

MEMORIAL

This photo of a double Memorial DOLMEN (among many) was located on the "GOLAN HEIGHTS" which at that time was occupied by Israel. The figure in the photo is my guide Rafael Carese. Rafael was born in Vermont as was I, but he migrated to Israel where he started his family.

Our trip, beginning at 4 am, was from Jerusalem, North around Sea of Galilee and up the mountain to **the Golan Heights.** After surveying the many monumental sites which most seemed to be family dolmen, we went to a restaurant to eat.

Over the horizon by the tree tops seen in the distance are the remains of the 1st Jewish Revolt (about 76 A.D.) against the Romans. In back of me, at some distance, is located a current mountain observatory, manned by an Israeli soldier.

About sunset we started our return trip South to Jerusalem. We went down to the Sea of Galilee level, turned South and followed the East side of the Jordan river. At that time of year it was really more like a brook. We arrived in Jerusalem about midnight ending a long but rewarding trip.

Dolmen and Raphal *Carese* on *Golan* Heights, Israel

MEMORIAL

The size of this Memorial DOLMEN indicates a large amount of energy was involved to place this boulder in this position. It is a huge "Table Rock" supported by two smaller stones thus qualifying it as a DOLMEN.

The human energy expended here and its location indicates a large catastrophe possibly a shipwreck. This memorial is just above a cove with a surrounding beach, on a peninsula which juts out into the Atlantic Ocean. It is on the Northwest coast of Portugal near the fishing village of Buru.

Dr Warren L. Cook, my companion on this trip, was explaining to our local guide, about the relevance of the stone chambers near by. Seeing these men by the stone indicates the size of this monument which tells us of its importance. However, the locals consider it "just another boulder."

Dolmen on the Atlantic Coast at Buru, Portugal.
Dr. Warren Cook and local guide in the background.

WRITING

The beginning of written communication seems to be in GRAPHIC STORY FORM. This example of a ŚUMER (Shumer) story board form of writing was located in the back of the British Museum when I went searching for it. This and many other examples **of GRAPHIC** displays were per-historic forms of communication.

I took this picture in 1974 while on a trip around Europe with my wife, Ruby. Thanks to the 1.5 years I spent indexing this photographic collection I was able to locate this image very easily and found the color was still very good.

Among the early forms of communication after GRAPHIC story telling came symbols representing sound values, or phonetics. These were generally made up of consonants with no vowels at first.

Phoenician, OGAM, Tifinag, and Cuneiform are examples of vowel-less alphabets. It is possible that due to the necessity in trading that these alphabets developed earlier than the more literary ones such as Aramaic, Hebrew and Greek.

An ancient Śumer (Shumer) story board housed in the British Museum in London, England

WRITING

Due to the efforts of having the French Emperor Napoleon's army build a fort in the Delta of the Nile River a memorial was found in late 1799. This memorial in three languages became named "THE ROSETTA STONE"

Numerous individuals endeavored to decipher this linguistic treasure but were unsuccessful until a young Frenchman, Jean Francois Champoll, identified the three alphabets, Hieroglyphs, Demotic and Greek. All three alphabets described the same memorial dedication.

Soon after the French liberated this wonderful "Rosetta Stone" from Egypt the English liberated it from the French and it eventually came to reside in the British Museum. It was there in 1974 when I was about 63 years old that I held the camera high over my head, guessed at the settings and took this picture. Unfortunately it isn't as sharp as I would like

The Rosetta Stone from Egypt
Three Languages in Three Alphabets
Now displayed in the British Museum in London

WRITING

3 ALPHABETS

This Photograph of the TRI-ALPHABETIC TABLET of the **OGAM** alphabet plus 3 of 5 diphthongs, with the equivalent in ancient Qufic Arabic alphabet and Egyptian Hieroglyphs is a copy of a snapshot by Mrs. Brenda Sullivan used with her permission. I first saw this snapshot in 1980 when Mrs. Sullivan and I were on a trip with the Epigraphic Society traveling up the Nile in Egypt.

Mrs. Sullivan photographed this stone from Sanuci Credo Mutwa's collection of inherited artifacts from a long line of ancestral Zulu Sanuci Healers in South Africa. (due to our ignorance we often call them "Witch Doctors").

This stone is a copy of an original given to Credo Mutwa when he, after working with his grandfather for years, graduated to become a Zulu Sanuci Healer and Historian. He is knowledgeable in several pre ancient alphabets and languages as well as English, Latin, Greek, Hebrew, Spanish, French and others. Credo was brought up by his mother and grandfather. Upon reaching an age to enter high school his father enrolled him in a catholic school so that he had the benefit of both cultures.

Credo was most gracious to me while I was visiting South Africa. He had his associates collect and place upon a large white canvas a number of his Zulu family artifacts for me to photograph. This particular tri-alphabetic tablet was with another exhibit.

Three Alphabets: Ogam, Kufic Arabic and Egyptian Hieroglyphs from Credo Mutwa's Zulu Collection in South Africa

WRITING

SIX ALPHABETS

In the latter part of the 5th century B.C. the renowned Historian ***Herodotus,*** while reviewing information given him by Egyptian Priests about Phonetians circum navigating the continent then known as EGYPT (Africa) commented; "While facing toward land I doubt that the sun sets over ones left shoulder". This was in reference to ancient traders visiting South Africa. This author checked out this phenomena while on a trip there in 1985 and saw that Herodotus was incorrect and the Egyptian Priests were correct in their History.

The *GOLD* ***TRADING STONE*** (from Zulu Sanuci Healer & Historian Credo Mutwa's family Artifact collection) exhibits six (6) different ancient ALPHABETS and an opening where the gold was placed for measuring. This orifice represented the vagina of MOTHER EARTH, giving her credit for furnishing the gold to trade.

The ancient era alphabets did NOT have vowels or diphthongs. The 5 alphabets and 1 symbol (the STAR OF DAVID representing the Hebrew Alphabet) are Tifinag, OGAM, Linear A, Egyptian Hieroglyphs, and ancient Greek.

I have photographed examples of one of these alphabets, OGAM (which was used in trade and related to the religion of the God Baal), numerous times in Africa, Asia Minor, Europe, South America and North America. From the number and distribution of these examples we can assume that the ancient world was well known and well traveled. By the way, OGAM and the later 4th century B.C. version, OgHam, which included vowels, were the forerunners of the current BAR CODE.

Zulu Gold Trading Stone with Five Alphabets (Ogam, Tifinag, Linear A, Ancient Greek and Egyptian Hieroglyphs) and the Star of David Symbol From Credo Mutwa's Collection in South Africa

WRITING

DIVINATION
by
ETRUSCANS

In some per Christian time an individual by name of **TAGES** compiled at least three (3) corpuses about **DIVINATION** or **PROPHESYING** related to the early Etruscan culture. These catalogues of laws of Divination or Prophecy were related to information called *LIBRI TAGETICI,* derived from LIGHTNING, ENTHRALLS OF ANIMALS and the FLIGHT OF BIRDS.

This practice of predicting by the Etruscans began about 3,000 B.C. and continued to about 600 B.C. *when it was discontinued.* These three collections of DIVINATIONS were taught to the LUCUMONES (HIGH PRIESTS) of the 12 City States of the Eutria area of what is now central Italy.

The Lucumones or High Priests who specialized in DIVINATION were called HARUSPICIERS and dealt with people or groups who had problems and needed counsel.

Etruria was ideally situated specifically for interpreting the DIVINATION of BIRDS in flight. It is on one of the most heavily traveled flyways of migrating fowl between Africa, Holland and Belgium. Birds flying in various fashion may be interpreted by Haruspicers as GOOD OR BAD OMENS.

Though **Columbus** was the great developer of the AMERICAS he was preceded in this area by many others, not by hundreds of years, but by CENTURIES.

Many of the early explorers were more highly developed than they have been given credit. The early ***OLMEC*** people had the DECIMAL system way before the highest EUROPEAN cultures acquired it.

The ancient ***ETRUSCAN EXPLORERS*** were another culture that traveled over thousands of miles to penetrate extensively into the ***North AMERICAN continent.*** It was at the ***Milk River,*** in Alberta, Canada that they left sculptured figures and inscriptions.

MAP
of
Central Italy
Called
ETRURIA

The ancient 12 City states of the area occupied by the ancient ETRUSCAN culture was approximately from what is now ROME to PISA along the western cost of Italy to the north. This area extended easterly across the peninsula with the present city of Florence (Firenze) in the north central portion.

Shipping and trade with other countries was conducive because this area of the country was exposed on both the East and West to seaports. Trade was especially active with the Phoenicians and Greeks around the Adriatic and Mediteranean Seas. The Etruscans were known to have also traded outside the Mediterranean area to as far away as Ireland, England and the Canary Islands. These islands served as Columbus' last stop before venturing further West to the Caribbean.

Early Home of Ancient Etruscans

INSCRIBED

ETRUSCAN

Bronze Mirror

6–4th Century BC

On the back of this 6th to 4th century B.C. Etruscan bronze mirror are two figures interacting. One is the Goddess Minerva who seems to be giving instructions to her companion. The second figure armed with a large war club seems ready to do battle.

It is important to notice the inscription in the Etruscan language written in the OGAM alphabet on Minerva staff. This indicates the use of this alphabet in the Etruscan culture in the 6th B.C. An even earlier example will be presented later in this book in the form of a 9th century B.C. HUT URN.

Etruscan 6–4th Century Inscribed Bronze Mirror.
Manervia instructing an Associate. Vowel-less Ogam is visible on her staff. Photo purchased from the British Museum in London.

SCULPTURES

A METHOD OF COMMUNICATION

This exquisite white marble sculptured statue by Michelangelo Buonsrroti is an excellent example of his ability to perform sculpturing as a means of communicating the majesty of DAVID, King of Israel.

Michelangelo Buonarroti was born within about an hour and a half drive from ancient "*Firenze*" now called Florence in northern Etruscany. Also the white marble for this sculpture came from this same area of Etruscany, Italy.

The talent and custom for sculpturing by the people of Etruscan birth used to communicate will be revealed later in this GRAPHIC NARRATIVE.

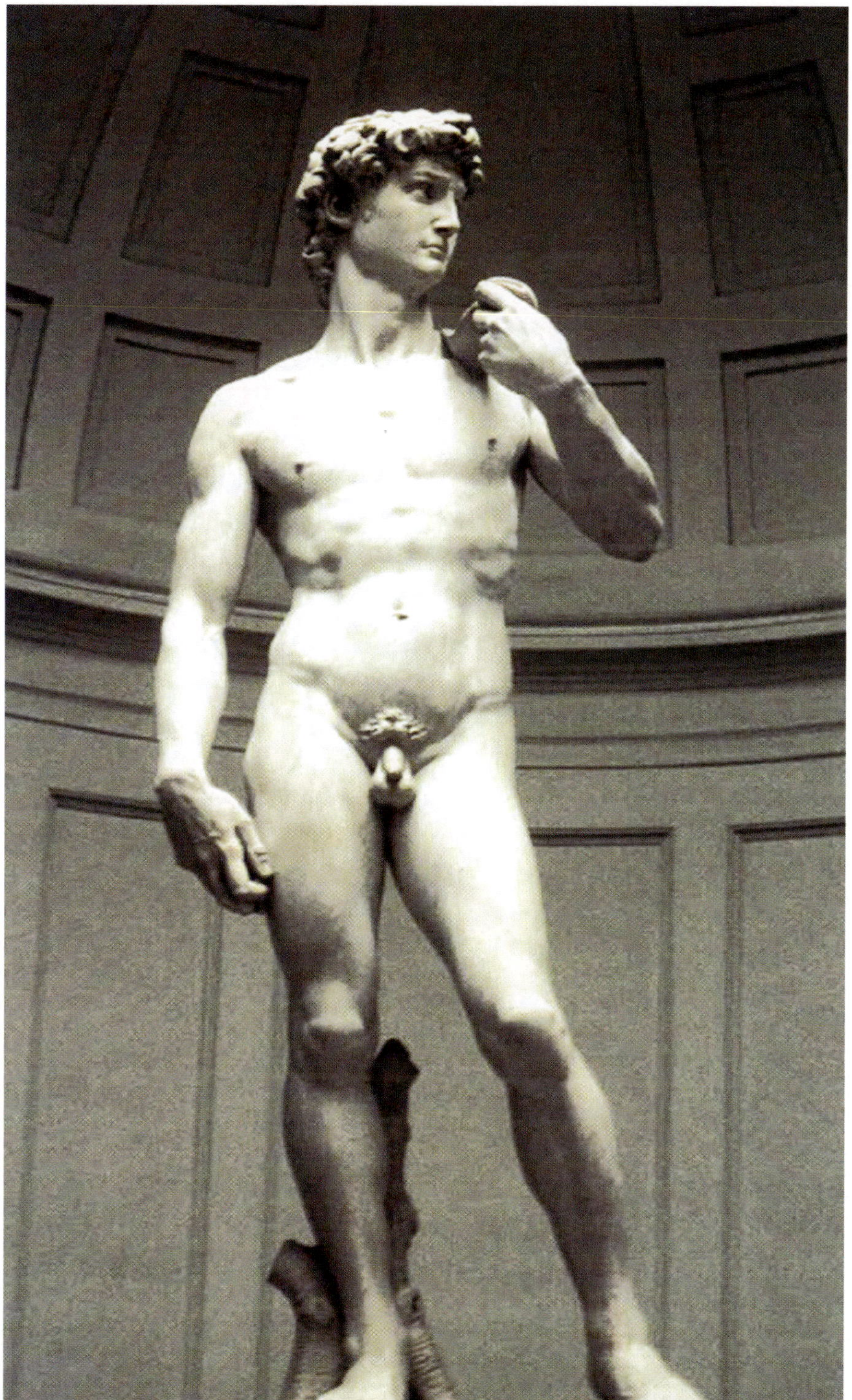

King David by Michelangelo Buonarroti
This statue is on display in Rome

SCULPTURES

FUNERAL BRASSES

In a number of European countries and especially in the British Isles, a custom of the wealthy was to have IMAGES of the departed loved ones SCULPTED IN BRASS and placed over their burial sites.

A newer custom has developed that takes advantage of these BRASS sculptures to make images of them. This process is known as "BRASS RUBBING" whereby a thin layer of stout paper **is laid over the BRASS and rubbed with a colored hard wax. This reproduces the original image.**

Brass rubbing from a church in England

SCULPTURES

MEMORIALS

This sculptured memorial CROSS in the Boic Monastery in Ireland is a beautiful example of the art of sculpture used to communicate a story.

The opportunity to photograph this exquisite artifact of a religious culture was while on a trip with my wife Ruby in 1974 Seldom are the desired photographic subjects lit by sunlight to show them at just the right way and the correct angle as this one was.

Sculpturing has long been a method of conveying a message and is a part of this GRAPHIC story as further revelations will show.

Sculptured Celtic Cross from Boic, Monaster, Ireland

SCULPTURES

BURIAL HUT URNS

Disseminating information by sculpting was a common means in ancient times. Symbols and words were used to pass on information of those whose ashes were contained in the hut urn.

The anchor on the front of this hut urn tells us that this individual was probably a sailor.

This particular Hut Urn is found in a museum in Guimaraes, Portugal

Hut Urn from Guimaraes Museum in Portugal

S C U L P T U R E S

HUT URNS

THE ***Unusual*** *(3 vertical lines)* ***raised symbols*** above the door on this 6th to 4th Century B.C. Etruscan Hut Urn spells out the name of the ancient Canaanite God, Baal, in the vowel-less **OGAM** alphabetic. The name of the God Baal is mentioned many times in the Old Testament of the King James version of the Holy Bible.

This unusual feature of raised Ogam letters has been ***found only in two locations, Etruria, Italy and on the Milk River in North AMERICA*** as future GRAPHICS will show.

This photo was purchased from the Swedish museum in Rome.

A 6th–4th Century B.C. Etruscan Hut Urn with raised Ogam letters above the door listing the name of the God Baal

S C U L P T U R E S

HUT URNS

From **Tomb #2500** in Pontecagnano (Salerno, Italy) is a **9th century** B.C. Etruscan Hut Urn. Recently this ancient Urn was in the Museo dell' Agro Picentino. This Hut Urn is also shown on page 241 of the Getty Publications ***"The Etruscans Outside Euteria."***

Above the front door and on the roof of this urn is another example of this ***UNUSUAL form of the OGAM alphabet*** *in raised letters. This spells out the name of the ancient Canaanite God Baal.* In this author's experience this SCULPTURED or raised letter form has been found only in two places, namely Eturia (Italy) and in only one place in North America.

9th Century B.C. Etruscan hut urn used for cremated ashes. The name of the God Baal is above the door in Ogam as well as on the roof. This hut urn is now in a museum in Italy.

ANCIENT FORMS OF COMMUNICATION

A partial list of ancient communication styles include:

1. **Sculptured figures**
   - Communicating through size and location

2. **"Dolmen" as Monuments**
   - Variety in the use of local materials
   - Size in relationship to importance

3. **Examples of the ancient vowel-less alphabet called OGAM**
   - Inscribed and in raised letters

4. **Ancient texts on stone display the blessings of the god Baal**
   - Hut Urns
   - Bronze Mirror
   - Dolmen

5. **Prophesying the future (Divination)**
   - Observing the flight of migrating birds

Fr. Carlo Crespi & Dr. Warren Cook in Ecuador, South America

Grave Cover Stone from Spain

Credo Mutwa a Zulu Historian & Healer

Baal in Ogam from Turkey

Signs of the Zodiac from Israel

Signs of the Zodiac from Ecuador, South America

10 Commandment Stone From South Africa

RIVERS

into

North America

Prior to Roman take over of Etruria, a number of Etruscan sailors became pirates and according to historian Strabo, they attempted to occupy the Canary Islands. These Islands are about 60 miles off the Northwest coast of Africa, This attempt was thwarted by the PHOENETIANS from Cartage.

The reason for mentioning this is because these islands were valuable to many cultures as a supply port. They served as the last stop that Christopher Columbus made before heading west. According to Italian History, Columbus was born at Genoa, Italy which is only a short distance from the ancient Etruscan West coast ports of Italy; It would be unusual if Columbus had not heard tales of Etruscans sailing "Beyond The Pillars of Gibralta".

After replenishing their supplies at the Canaries Islands and leaving toward the West they would have been helped by prevailing currents and winds. The ancient Etruscans would have traversed the Caribbean, the Gulf of Mexico and entered the mouth of the Mississippi River. The abundant resources available would have provided a great incentive for further exploration up stream. The Mississippi would lead them to the Missouri and further on to the Milk River (named "Milk River" by Lewis and Clark during their 1805 expedition).

This hand drawn map of the principal rivers of North America shows the potential for extensive penetration into the continent. This mode of water travel was very familiar to the ancient Etruscans. The river system would furnish ample food and water for such explorers.

The Etruscans, exploring North and West, found a prominent area on the high bluffs above the Milk River where they left written and sculptured messages of their presence and culture.

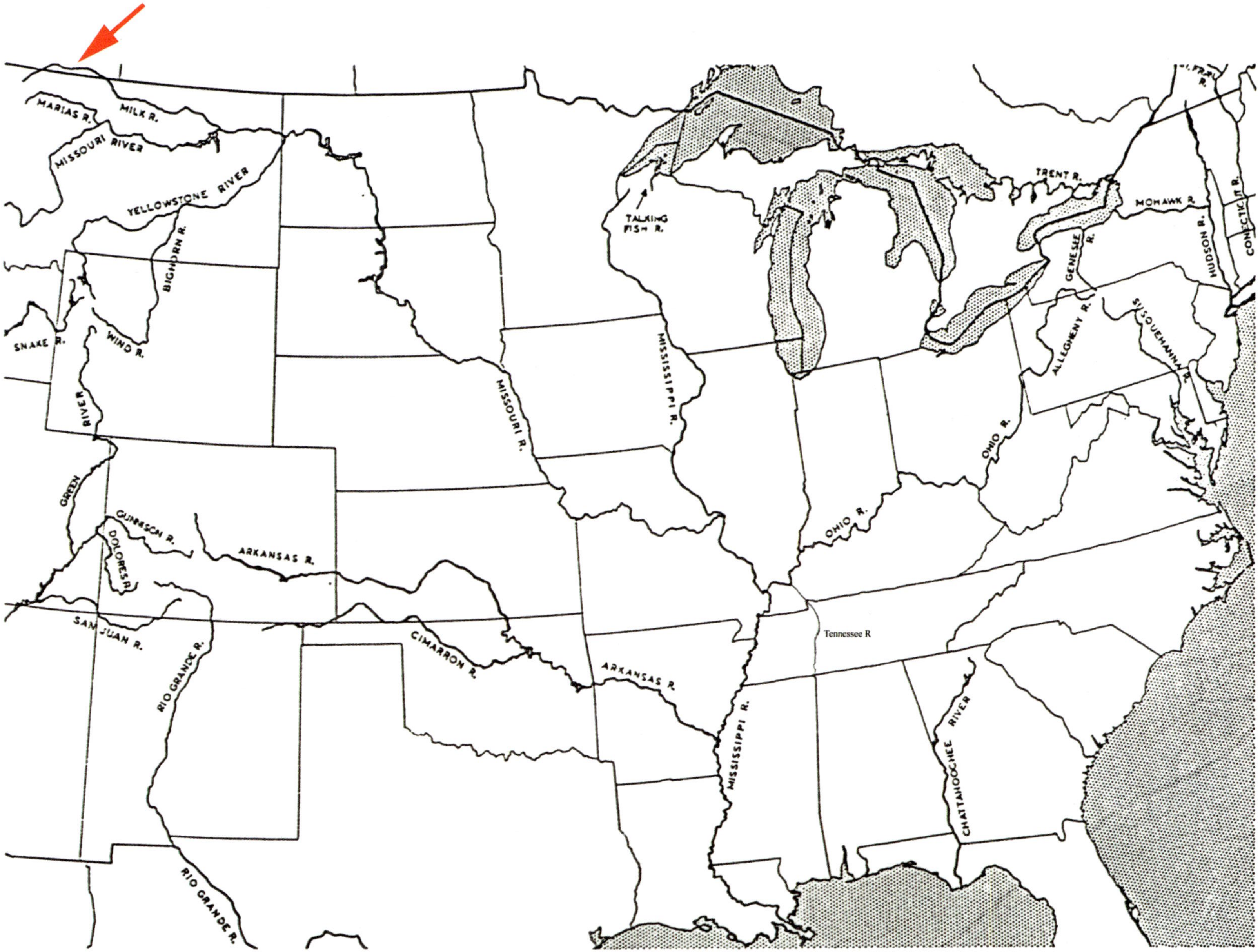

Rivers into North America which were used by the ancient explorers as highways

Raised OGAM Letters

Sculptured Dolmen From a "HODO"

Back in 1989 I was fortunate to acquire a long focal length lens (1500mm) which allowed this photograph to be taken from the western end of WRITING on STONE Provincial Park. This park is located beside the Milk River in Southern Alberta, Canada. The Dolmen was at least a mile away from where I was standing. From this angle the *raised letters* of the OGAM alphabet show up thanks to the sun light.

It wasn't until this image was processed that the RAISED LETTER OGAM was recognized and the relationship to another site, upriver, was realized. The other location will be shown presently.

The size of the DOLMEN and the religious connotation of the ***unusual** raised letter* form of the (vowel-less) OGAM alphabet *naming the ancient Canaanite God BaaL indicates a monument to a valued leader.* As the information from these sites unfolds it would seem that THE ETRUSCAN EXPLORERS had reached this area and established a working site long before the Christian era.

A monument in the form of a Dolmen with the Raised Ogam Letters naming the God Baal. It is conspicuously located on a cliff above the Milk River in Alberta, Canada.

SCULPTURED OGAM

(Raised Letter Form)

A close up of this raised letter OGAM reveals its age by showing the erosion.

The ETRUSCANS, after cremation, buried the ashes of their deceased in HUT URNS with the name of BaaL on it in raise letter OGAM. Centuries after the original explorers, assumed to be ETRUSCANS, the Indian people came and established their societies. They, too, needed a place of security for their deceased members. The Indians found a secure place on top of the ETRUSCAN'S MONUMENTAL DOLMEN, where the tightly bound bodies of the deceased were laid to rest until their flesh disappeared. After about a year the medicine men of the tribe reclaimed the remaining bones and buried them elsewhere.

Above the OGAM writing is an ***Eagle Mask*** of the lead Medicine man of the BEAR tribe, sculptured into the dolmen. This was done to protect the sanctity of the sacred site. At the other end of the top of the dolmen is the sculptured snout or face of a bear, representing the INDIAN clan.

<u>Raised Ogam Letters</u> on the Dolmen
above the Milk River in Alberta, Canada

Sculptured FACES Caucasian and Negroid

OGAM writing vowel-less Alphabet

DIVINATION Prophesying by The flight Pattern of BIRDS

The MILK RIVER PILLAR site is a story board of GRAPHIC information left behind by very ancient explorers believed to be the Etruscans.

In 1982 I was privileged to have Lawrence Helmrest of Southern Alberta (seen standing behind the pillar) guide me with his friend Robert Bear (standing to the left) to this exquisite sight. *This is the MOST outstanding of all the* sites along the Milk River in Alberta . . . yet it was not among those sites that had been documented or photographed that I could find in my research. I was delighted to be taken there.

I greatly appreciated the courtesy extended to me allowing me to do research in the Lethbridge City Library, The Calgary Museum (where I spent 2 days in their top floor archive) and for information about *Writing on Stone* Provincial Park by the Alberta Archaeological Society.

After I saw this was NOT accepted as a site worth saving I wrote a number of letters which included this photograph, asking WHY something was not done to preserve it. I wrote to The Canadian National Parks Department in Ottawa whose response was to "contact the local Parks Department". The local parks department sent out an *ENGINEER* who said the river would eventually undermine the whole cliff so nothing could be done about it. I also contacted a local Lethbridge University Archaeological Professor who seemed to be interested but didn't even go to see the site. Next, I wrote letters to the editors of three of the largest newspapers in Alberta with no acknowledgement or publicity. I recognize the possibly of my being a "dam Yankee" kiboshed my appeal.

The story revealed in this photograph is *that two faces, a Caucasian and a Negro were sculptured* to let posterity know who had been there, The Negro sculpture looks similar to the OLMAC relics left in Central America by ancient Negroes from Africa. The high position of the Caucasian sculptured figure in respect to the Negroid figure, could indicate LEADERSHIP by the former.

The Third and very important feature is the *Ancient (vowel-less) OGAM alphabetic inscription on the pillar.* This inscription as deciphered by Dr. Barry Fell, is a duplicate of the DIVINATION or prediction of the future as preached by priests in ancient Etruscans' homeland of Etruria, Italy.

Ogam inscribed pillar above the Milk River in Alberta, Canada

OGAM
Inscribed Writing

DIVINATION
On The
Milk River
Alberta, Canada

The message inscribed on the SANDSTONE pillar is in the vowel-less OGAM alphabet and is translated as a DIVINATION or PROPHECY of the future. This prediction is determined by the flight pattern of the migrating BIRDS.

Divination was a common practice in the ancient Etruscan Culture taught by their priests before the Christian era.

Lawrence Helmrest of Warner, Alberta, Canada, my guide to this site is shown behind the Pillar. Unfortunately, he is now deceased.

The body of the Ogam Pillar above the Milk River in Alberta, Canada.
Lawrence Helmrest, our guide, is shown in the back right.

OGAM WRITING DECIPHERED

From the Milk River Alberta, Canada

by

Dr. Barry Fell

Here is the actual breakdown and working DECIPHERMENT of the message in the vowel-less OGAM alphabet by Dr. Barry Fell. This message was inscribed in the so called "OGAM PILLAR", on the high bluff above the Milk River, about 10 miles, into Alberta, above the U. S. & Canadian border.

The decipherment reveals the use of the flight of migrating birds between Central and South America and Alaska. Their flight pattern was the basis for the prophesy or divination about the future.

The "Libri TAGETICI" a collection of three books by TAGUS, describe the rules for the priests to make predictions into the future from LIGHTNING, from INWARDS of wild beasts, and from the FLIGHT pattern of BIRDS.

This Divination procedure is the SAME both here in ancient North America and where it originated in the ancient ETRUSCANS' homeland, ETURIA, Italy

This amazing decipherment by Dr. Barry Fell was made possible by the use of a montage of several photos encompassing the whole inscription around the pillar, taken by the author in 1982.

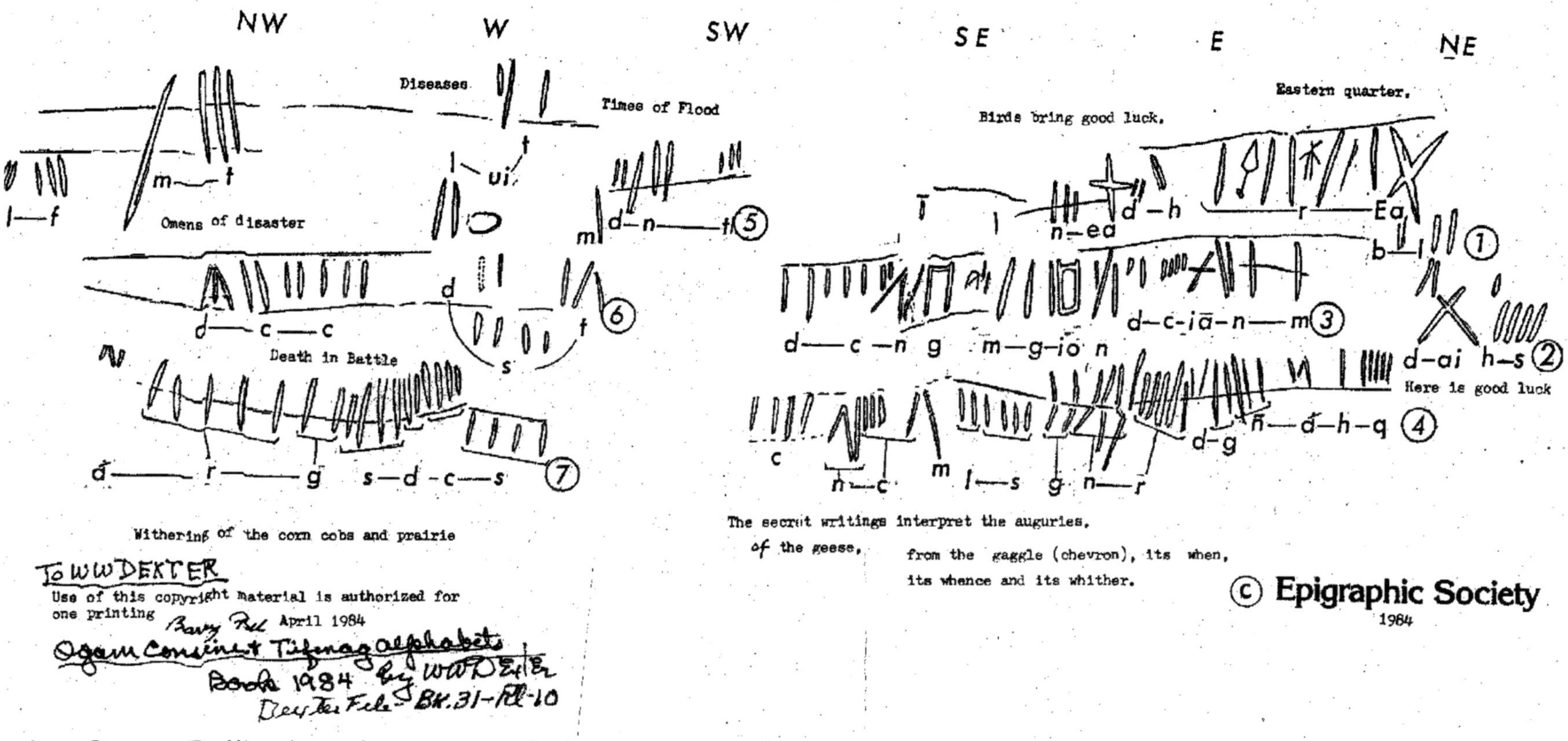

Dr. Barry Fell's decipherment of the message found on the Ogam Pillar above the Milk River in Alberta, Canada. The message reveals the subject of divination similar to those messages used by the Etruscans in ancient Italy. Permission to use this was purchased from Mrs. Rene Fell, Secretary of E.S.O.P., shortly after Barry's death.

TWO SCULPTURED HEADS

Over Look The Milk River In Alberta, Canada

The Negro (Olmec) Head

The sculptured NEGRO head accompanying the Caucasian sculptured head, atop the OGAM Pillar, is similar to the Olmec sculptured figures found elsewhere, generally in Central America. Since one figure is placed below the other it would be consistent with other sites and sculptures as an indication of subservience. It could be assumed the Caucasian to be the leader and the Negro to be of less social status or even a servant. Those who worked as servants and slaves were vital to the expedition. Even though the explorers traveled mainly by way of the rivers it was a strenuous journey with much heavy lifting.

The SCULPTURING of these two figures is a continuation of ancient customs of conveying information via sculptured story scenes.

The Negro Sculptured Face located by the
Ogam Pillar above the Milk River in Alberta, Canada.

TWO SCULPTURED HEADS

Over Look The Milk River
In Alberta, Canada

The Caucasian Head

I first photographed the OGAM PILLAR and the sculptured CAUCASIAN HEAD in 1982. Even though it was badly eroded by age it still showed the features of a white person assumed to be a representation of an Etruscan based upon the style and content of the OGAM message.

Because of its height above the NEGROID sculptured head it is also assumed that this figure represented the leader of the expedition.

The Sculptured Caucasian Head of the Ogam Pillar
above the Milk River in Alberta, Canada. Photo taken in 1982.

VANDALS STRIKE

Irreparable damage to the Sculptured Caucasian Head Above MILK RIVER Alberta, Canada

Upon revisiting the Milk River in 1998 I was disheartened to find that descendants of the VANDALS who in ancient times had so decimated North Africa, were up to their destructive activities at this important site. Two sculptured head site above MILK RIVER.

The bullet holes in the remains, reveals that the VANDALS of some culture, had user the sculptured head on the bluff about 65 ft, above Milk River as a target, demolishing the face completely.

In the summer of 2004 the author received a call from a friend in Alberta with bad news. "THE NEGRO SCULPTURED HEAD had fallen into the river due to the spring freshest undercutting its support."

From hereon it is up to the reader:

TO accept the assumptions of this book or reject them.

TO work in the future trying to preserve ancient remains of all kinds !

Damage by vandals to the Ogam Pillar shown in a 1998 photograph